FOUND

FOUND

A Collection of Poems from a Broken Heart

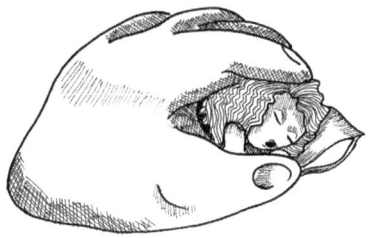

T. M. Mackie

Edited by Belinda Love
Illustrated by Echo Phillips

RESOURCE *Publications* • Eugene, Oregon

FOUND
A Collection of Poems from a Broken Heart

Copyright © 2022 T. M. Mackie. All rights reserved. Except for brief quotations in critical publications or reviews, no part of this book may be reproduced in any manner without prior written permission from the publisher. Write: Permissions, Wipf and Stock Publishers, 199 W. 8th Ave., Suite 3, Eugene, OR 97401.

Resource Publications
An Imprint of Wipf and Stock Publishers
199 W. 8th Ave., Suite 3
Eugene, OR 97401

www.wipfandstock.com

PAPERBACK ISBN: 978-1-6667-4219-0
HARDCOVER ISBN: 978-1-6667-4220-6
EBOOK ISBN: 978-1-6667-4221-3

JULY 5, 2022 10:56 AM

For my mother. A promise kept.

Also dedicated to the organisation Women's Aid, whose tireless work and care help so many reach a place of safety and peace.

Contents

Foreword | *ix*

Introduction | *xi*

Lost and Found | 1

Love Covers | 2

My Testimony | 3

Sin | 4

Being Cuddled | 5

The Question | 7

No Hiding Place | 8

Help is at Hand | 9

Saving Grace | 10

Surrender | 11

I Am | 13

A Soaring Golden Eagle | 14

Dear Echo | 15

Fallen Short | 16

Thank You | 18

Smile | 19

The Foolishness of Man – The Wisdom of God | 20

A Bruised Reed | 21

Blood | 22

Paid For | 23

With You in Mind | 25

Be Mine, I Know Your Name | 26

Perfectly Loved | 27

His Saving Grace | 29

Lord Renew My Mind | 30

Hand in Hand | 31

Arise, Arise | 32

Think Not Higher Than You Ought | 33

Sisters | 34

His Faithfulness | 35

Gems | 36

Foreword

By Belinda Love

Becoming a survivor of a traumatic experience is a personal journey through oneself. One can travel through many versions of themself and discover new ones. Some of these versions can be ugly, unfamiliar, and chaotic. Hard to face, understand, and show to anyone.

One can travel through their whole life in one day, one hour, one moment; from childhood to what looks like the possible end of everything. But survive, many do. These are the brave souls. These are the souls who should speak and be listened to. They have stories to tell. They say words that matter. Their words are soaked in harsh reality, truth, and learned wisdom.

Following, is a collection of poems written by my mother over many years while she lived and suffered in an abusive relationship. Alcoholism, manipulation, violence, destruction, homelessness, child neglect, despair, fear; financial, emotional, and sexual abuse. A sadly typical list that some of you may find familiar.

Her relationship with herself evolved gradually as she absorbed the relentless drip-fed negative energy and found new ways of coping. Bad and good. Alcoholism is a well-known coping mechanism for suffering anxiety and stress. But the ending there is not usually a happy one. During a particularly low point my mother was found unconscious in the street and was aided by two passing born-again Christians. They took her in, showed her care

Foreword

and kindness, listened to her; and told her she was welcome, loved, and safe. Isn't that all any of us wants?

She joined their group and attended their gatherings, and the enrichment she felt in their celebrating of life and God and love gave her new strength and joy, bringing back a sparkle to her eyes that I feared was long gone. Bringing her back to life. She stumbled upon peace while living in turmoil.

My mother's individual relationships with her children suffered over this time as they each struggled to understand the whys and wherefores. Why she stayed, seemingly forsaking them. They journeyed through their own evolutions and recoveries over the years, trying to make sense of the insensible.

My own relationship with my mother was difficult through this time. Anger, abandonment, and frustration were ongoing themes in the counselling I undertook to try to understand. Eventually she did leave her situation, having reached her own limit. Twenty-eight years it took. She fled far away and spent some happy years living on her own for the first time in her life. Just being herself and making new friends easily in Christian worship groups. She then suffered a mini stroke and developed vascular dementia and Alzheimer's, which she now slowly disappears into. These ailments taught me great patience and empathy, and after my own heart was abused, I came to realise that she was and had always been just a broken-hearted woman trying to survive. But her poems are intact and remain.

She wrote these poems to log and emulate her feelings, stories, and cherish her newly found joy and safety. She and I began collating the poems over a decade ago to put them into a collection and seek publication, but the unpredictability of life and ill health encumbered that project. We are now delighted to finish that task, and we are grateful to Resource Publications for their interest in publishing them.

Even in darkness, light can be found.

Introduction

Meaning can be better understood, interpreted, or felt, by having access to some context. When collating this collection, two forgotten journals belonging to my mother were among her poems. These are from the last few months before she fled. Within these excerpts is some context. They are not dramatic. Like the frog in gradually increasing hot water, it either realises it's too hot, or, it doesn't. For privacy, the names have been changed. Except for my own.

> **29th June** - Went home. Very quiet. Barry looks really awful. Peaceful night. Men came to fit shower. Barry gave me all the money, had me buy whisky, put a bet on dogs. I talked to him about Vanessa he said that sounded like a word John would use and said I could say it, could I spell it. I said even if I could not spell it, I knew what it meant. Why did he say that?
>
> **30th June** - Did not want to row. Rang Mary to say would be late. Worked getting things out of cupboard so men could work to do shower. Very hot. Barry in and out of bed a lot. Did not eat anything. Not well.
>
> **2nd July** - Barry managed to eat dinner. Praise God quiet night.
>
> **4th July** - Nice hot day again. Barry not well. Getting gobby again. He did manage to eat dinner. In and out of bed all day. He is really not well.

Introduction

5th July - Nice day going to church. Did some shopping on the way home. It rained a little. Barry feeling a bit better. Managed to eat something. Needed more whisky.

6th July - Steve's birthday. Went to P.O. paid bills. Got whisky. Barry made dinner. He's not happy so I am keeping my head down.

7th July - Up early at 6am. Good day housework wise. Shower room coming along nicely. Barry managed to eat. Still nasty with words. Sad like his mother. Help him please Lord.

8th July - Went to Mary's then into town. Barry still not feeling well. Poppy rang, Barry answered the phone, asked what it was about. I did not want to tell him. He did not ask again. He had a nice dinner but was sick later. Went to bed then got up and was sick again.

9th July - Went to Mary's. Barry angry. Says he will ring up demanding money. Went out to lunch. Nancy rang up, nice to talk to her. Things quiet when I got home. I got cards for babbies birthdays.

10th July - Up early. Made bread. Feel very tired today. Someone broke wall plate? I told Barry if he runs out of whisky and has no money I am not going to give him some of mine.

13th July - Row with Barry over money. He was nasty with words again. He went to P.O. for money. I went later to P.O. Barry not well. I had a good day, worked very hard in the house. Helped Mary today. I am going out tomorrow. Barry in bed a lot.

15th July - Went out with Hannah and clan to the Bright Centre. What a lovely day. I made dinner before I went out. Barry went to bed early (late for him). He did not have a good night.

Introduction

16th July - Went to Mary's. Did hand-washing before I went. Stayed late to do the tent. Looks good. Hope it works well on Saturday. Barry upset because I was late back. I cut his hair yesterday, it looks very nice.

17th July - Worked in house doing paint work on landing and hanging pictures on the walls. Looks lovely. Went to prayer meeting at Sarah's. Good meeting. Barry in bed when I got home.

18th July - Did outreach. Got Barry some whisky. Did some shopping. Barry made my dinner. Omelette and chips. Very nice.

20th July - Went to P.O. got the money, paid electric. Got whisky for Barry. He is not happy about money again. First he does not want it, then he wants it. Plumber came to finish the shower room. He put bolt on for me. Barry still angry and rude and insulting. He goes to bed very early. TV won't work again so I go to bed early too.

22nd July - Called on Clare but she was out so walked to Mary's. Then went to town to get blades for mower. Barry went for a lay down. I am going to look after the twins in Aug/Sep. Barry okay about it.

24th July - Up early and had a shower. Did my prayer hour. Read newspaper. Went to post letters. Barry not up to doing any gardening but up to rowing and being nasty after having a so-called lay down. I made nice dinner, watched TV then went to bed.

29th July - Barry went on again about HD box. I do not want to get one yet. He just will not see my point of view on things and then gets very nasty and really hurts my feelings. Insults me and bosses me about. Enjoy my own company more and more.

Introduction

30th July - Barry sees nothing wrong with anything he says or does. I am so tired. Went to Mary's, Hannah was there. Told her about my missing things. I am so angry with myself for being so afraid of Barry. He put my things out of reach and now they are gone. I feel like Job who feared the worst and then it happened, so I trust the Lord to restore everything back to me.

31st July - Barry has got to stop criticising me all the time and foul insults it makes me so angry I shout back and it gets me nowhere. I work all day and night in my bedroom. Barry nasty again. Will be glad to go to Scotland. Barry made sweet just for himself. Turned TV off.

1st Aug - I have had another row with Barry and I have only been up half an hour. He needs money back for whisky. Must have HD box that's all I hear. He is being hateful and foul tempered. Only nice thing about today was Steve rang up. TV went off again, more bad temper.

2nd Aug - Wonderful time at church. Told Hannah the good news about finding my things, she had prayed for me to find them. What a blessing she is, love her very much. You are a God who never fails us. The one and only living God. Thanks that I had a restful day.

3rd Aug - Did my readings, gave thanks to the Lord for this new day. Went to P.O. got money and paid bills. Got whisky, was longer than I thought I would. Barry slept well last night. Claims he gets angry because of lack of sleep, yet being bad tempered again grabbing at me, said I have to come upstairs out of the way. It's 1:45 pm. I got the little bedroom sorted out, mine not finished yet. Keep getting more stuff for charity shop. Got an upset tummy. Barry is still angry. He does not like his life. He does not know how to enjoy anything.

5th Aug - First thing went round town with Mary, enjoyed going round the town. Phoned Sarah, she is off to

Introduction

New York with Nancy and Ray. She will see Trevor and give him a big hug for me.

6th Aug - Barry had a good rest last night. I don't see the point in me having any conversation with Barry because no matter what words I choose they are wrong. I thank him for showing me how to work the VCR. I feel really ill with his spiteful remarks and constant verbal abuse. Poppy looking forward to me coming up to look after twins. Thank you Lord for the friends you have given to Poppy. My bike has a puncture.

7th Aug - I stay in getting on with my bedroom. Think I have given wrong bag to charity shop. So angry with myself. I really need some quiet time. So hard to get time to myself. Too many things going round and round in my head. Finding it hard to forgive myself for getting things wrong.

9th Aug - Another row with Barry. Me losing my temper because of his lack of understanding in every way. Help him a little in the garden. I said I was sorry for what I said this morning, but he will not accept my saying sorry.

10th Aug - Hannah has her op today. What a horrible day. Barry for spite makes me pay Steve and phone bill and gives me nothing for TV. Tells me he does not love me anymore and he would leave me today if he had enough money and somewhere to go. Then he wonders why there is no peace or harmony in what should be our home. I must take care of myself and know that I am a dearly loved child of the living God.

11th Aug - Barry changing TV and phone over to Virgin. Was nasty even though he got his own way. Sad all he knows how to do is insult and lash out. Got on with my bedroom. Did some washing. Barry went to bed. I sorted out some things downstairs.

INTRODUCTION

15th Aug - Barry was up early. I went to do the puppet show. Weather was good, it went very well. Nice to see so many brothers and sisters in Christ. Did a bit of shopping. Then came home.

16th Aug - Woke up early. Wrote a poem then went back to sleep. Went to church and took newspaper back and got new one. Barry fixed my bike. He is not happy about anything. I did not rush home from church. Called in on Clare, so nice to see her, had a cup of tea. Barry just getting up as I get back. I go up and do my bedroom. I am very tired. Off to Scotland tomorrow. Wow I am so looking forward to it.

17th Aug - I get up early and do my packing. I tell Barry I'm taking my money with me. Tell him to enjoy the whisky from me. Good trip on the bus to Scotland. Met by Poppy and Belinda. Gerry is in hospital. Barry rang Poppy to say I'm not to bother ringing him up. Belinda did not stay long, she had to get back for Aaron.

18th Aug - I got up about 8am. Twins still asleep. Poppy having a lie in. I take her tea in bed and do girls' breakfast. Poppy having a morning off. Gerry on pain killers, no reports yet. Girls go to nursery. Catch up with my readings. Nice restful day. Jared helps with the twins. Chicken and salad for my dinner. Hope Barry had a good day.

27th Oct - Belinda woke me up. I got up just after she went to work and Aaron went to school. I did not do much before I went to Poppy's. Poppy went with me to see Karen at Women's Aid. I go back again on Thursday and go into refuge and start my new life. So very glad Poppy was with me. I know I will cry a lot. Have had so many hurts and my dear children too. Thank you Lord for answered prayers. Wrote a poem when I got back to Belinda's. Bought a pretty bag and a book with a rainbow.

Lost and Found

Underneath the surface, this is where he sees.
No act and mask; or part you play,
Can make the lost seem found.

Dying in the crowd. Who am I?
Doesn't anybody care?
Some people walk straight by.
Others only stare. Can't they see,
The pain I'm in?

The act has stopped.
The mask is broken.
The play's fallen apart.
At last, at last, he gives in.

Within his broken heart, a cry so deep,
So loud it came out like a sigh.
His Lord saw beneath the surface,
And healed his wounded heart.

Said, "Come follow me; we will never part.
I am the way, the truth, the life.
You were lost, but now you're found."

Love Covers

When "I love you" gets told to stuff it,
A tender little hug might be enough,
Just to keep you hanging on,
In a world of dark and cold.

When love is blind and marriage is an eye-opener,
Remember, love covers a multitude of sins.

When the baby's screaming in the middle of the night,
You are feeling about, one eye open, reaching for the light.
It's been going on for weeks.

You are oh so tired, and the window is so near,
You know you will not throw it out. You love the little dear.

Love covers all things and never fails.

My Testimony

Today ask, and it will be given unto you.
You do not have because you do not ask.

I was looking for something; calmly, I asked the Lord to help me
 find it.
I open a drawer in a set of drawers in my bedroom,
I moved two items, and there it was,
The very thing I was looking for.

How thankful I was, with praise and joy I gave thanks to my Lord,
Who is ever mindful of me, even over small things to bless me.

Sin

An argument going on inside.
A knocking at the door.
"I'll go; you stay put," he says.
I cannot hear what's being said.

I go stand by his side.
Policemen at the gate with guns.
"What's going on?" I cry.
We've come about your son, can we come inside.

Murder was the word they used.
No fear, alarm, just strangely numb.
Unreal, lost in time, I cannot say a word.
Baby running around the room, tea being made.

Made things normal in a way,
Yet we know the price that life has charged for us.
Victims and partakers in sins,
Both great and small.

Praise God that we have Jesus.
Forgiver of us all. That in him there is love,
That surpasses all understanding.

Being Cuddled

What colour is a cuddle? Is it pale blue?
Or is it like a blanket being wrapped around you?
A feeling of being surrounded by love.
Rest, let it happen, let him hold you,
In his everlasting loving arms.

He will hold you like no other, never letting you go.
He knows everything about you. He knows all there is to know.
Yet in love, he'll hold you and never leave you.

He calls, "Come to me, come to me,
All you who are weary, lost, and lonely.
Come, I will give you rest.
Do not be afraid; it is I".

"Come to me, come to me, if you're lonely.
Come to me, come to me, please do.
Come to me, come to me, if you're weary,
For my yoke is easy, and you will have rest.
Come to me as you are, just as you are.
Know the joy of being forgiven; come to me.

There is no charge; the gift is free.
Come oh come, come live in me.
The past is gone; you are set free.
When you come and give your life to me,
All things are made new; you will be mine.
I will never forsake you or leave you.

Come live in me, be a child of the living God.
Be holy, for I am holy. Lean not on your own.
Trust me, follow me; I am the Alpha and Omega.

We are Father, Son, and the Holy Spirit.
Come to me, come to me, I want that none should perish.
Like a little child, come. My arms are open, come.

The Lord is close to the broken-hearted,
And save those who are crushed in spirit.
I sought the Lord, and he answered me.
He delivered me from all my fears.
Taste and see that the Lord is good.
Blessed is he who takes refuge in him.

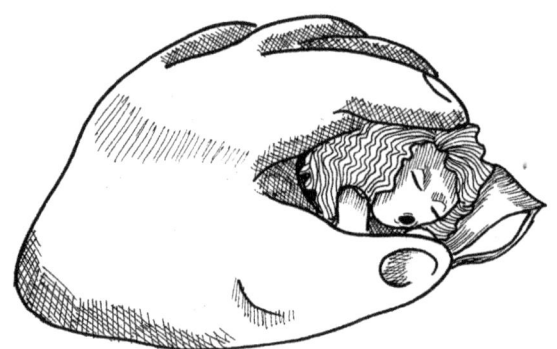

The Question

Will you not say guilty as charged when you are?
We all fall short of the glory of God.
This, is why we need to be redeemed, saved,
Rescued from the gates of Hell.
Turn around, stop going your own way,
Just because you can, with the gift of free will.

God so loved the world he gave his only
Begotten son Jesus, Prince of Peace, to die for you.
The question is: Who do you say Jesus is?
Do not ignore the question; it is directed at you.
Personally you cannot undo your sin.
Jesus has done all that needed to be done.
Paid in full for your forgiveness.

You will have to answer the question one day.
Better this side of Heaven. This is the day of your salvation.
No one knows if they will see another day.
The question is not unfair; it is real.
"Who do you say Jesus is?" Remember God wants
That none should perish. Hell is not made for Man but,
He can send himself there. Believe and receive salvation today.

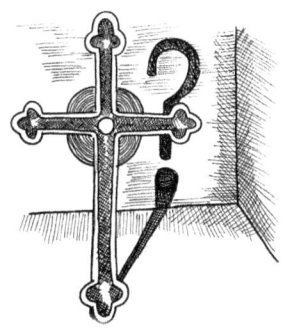

No Hiding Place

No hiding place for me from thee.
No darkness in thy sight.
Take me then and make me yours,
And bathe me in the light.

Your strength be mine, I might
Rest and hide myself in thee.
From the grace that comes from you,
And stills a desperate heart.

Come now and reside in me,
Nevermore to part.
Make me o Lord, live out the
Planned proposal in your heart.

Give birth to me again in you,
Please be the greater part.
That I in you, and you in me, never, ever, part.

May I submit all my heart,
That the plan you have for my life,
Will be live, and we will never part.

Help is at Hand

Lord put a guard over my mouth.
May I not be a stinker thinker.
Help me to meditate on your word.
Show me the way I should go.
For you have gone before me in all things.
You know the plans you have for me.

Your faithfulness is new every morning.
You have promised to finish what you have begun in me.
May I ever keep my eyes on you.
Thank you for your faithful servant Jesus,
Who obeyed you unto death, even death on the cross,
So that I received the gift of salvation.

Freely given to all who will believe in the name of Jesus.
God made flesh, the living word.
Crucified, risen from the dead.
Victory over sin and death.
Give thanks. This was done for you.
Glory be to God on high.

Saving Grace

Thank you, God, for who I am,
And that you made me, me.
Thank you, God, for your sweet grace,
That set my spirit free.

Thank you, God, for letting me see,
How much I mean to you.
That you should send your son to die,
For my sins instead of me.

I repent and with a grateful heart,
Give ever thanks to thee.
Amen.

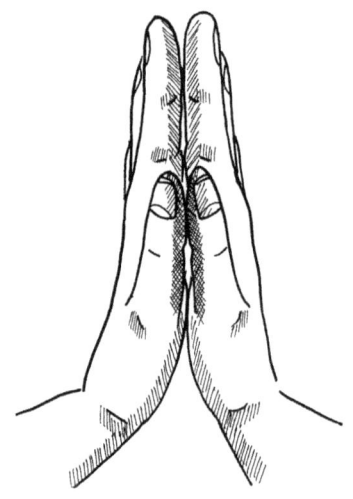

Surrender

Do you not know? Have you not heard?
Of the one who died for you?
Emptied himself of all but love,
Knowing all that you have done.

Crying to the Father, they know not what they do.
Blinded, naked, lost, alone, bound by sin and pride.
Not seeing the light of man incarnate Jesus,
Only-begotten, son of God.

Standing before the Father, arms open wide.
Calling to all who will have him as their Lord and saviour.
There is no other; these are the last days.
Fall on your knees, bless him, praise him, honour him in all you do.

He is the first and the last, put him first, trust him.
He will never fail you, leave you, or desert you. Rest in him.
He is the lover of your soul. Thank him for the gift of eternal life.
Thank God, the Father, Son, and Holy Spirit. Surrender to him.

Repent, be truly loved, receive the peace that supposes all
    understanding.
Only in the name of Jesus can you be made right with God.
For God so loved the world that he gave his only begotten son
    Jesus.
He gave him for you, the whomsoever, who will say yes and come
    to him.

God devised a perfect plan to reconcile the soul of Man.
Through Christ, the saviour come to Earth,
Revealed the gift of second Birth.
Gift of the Father through the Son. Sing hallelujah. Victory won.

I Am

I was regretting the past,
And fearing the future.
Suddenly my Lord was speaking.
"My name is I Am."

He paused.
I waited.
He continued.

"When you live in the past,
With its mistakes and regrets,
It is hard; I am not there.
My name is not I Was."

"When you live in the future,
With problems and fears,
It is hard; I am not there.
My name is not I Will Be."

"When you live in this moment,
It is not hard; I am here.
My name is I Am."

A Soaring Golden Eagle

Learning to rest in the Lord,
Like an eagle rests on the air.
Without effort soaring higher and higher.
Flight feathers like fingertips stretched out wide,
Getting higher and higher in the sky.

What a view to look down upon,
First above and then below.
His leg feathers looking like,
The baggy troosers cowboys
Wear in the films of long ago.

Thank you for the memories like this, Lord.
Lifting me up higher and higher with you.

Dear Echo

Welcome to the world,
Lovely little gift from God.
May the Prince of Peace reign in your heart.
Delight your parents.
Honour your father and mother,
So they will have a song in their hearts.
For the joy you give them.
The Lord has put an angel to watch over you.
Welcome, welcome, little child.

From Nana Toni xxx

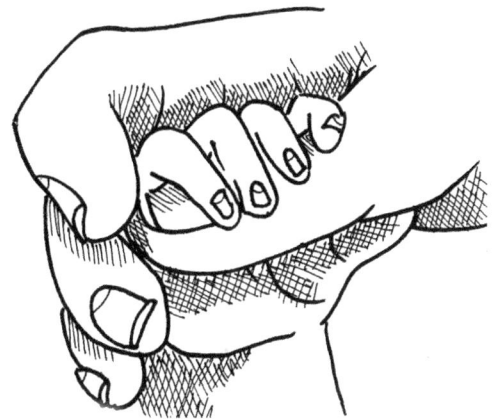

Fallen Short

Are you not tired of walking your own way?
Down the road of the lost, with your heavy burden of sin.
The lie you told yourself, that you are not a sinner.
We all have fallen short of the glory of God, yes you!

But there is good news; you have a saviour; Jesus is his name.
Sent by God and willingly he came, to die in your place.
For the wages of sin is death declared of the beginning.
For dust you are, and to dust will return.

Jesus offers you freely the gift of life, resurrection, new life in him.
The fool says in his heart there is no God;
The lie Satan wants you to believe.
So that you will lose out for all eternity.

God only sees the saved and the unsaved,
He wants that none shall perish.
Repent, turn now, say yes to Jesus.
He came that you might be saved.

If only you could understand, let the son of God take your hand.
Lead you in the way you should go, for he knows the plans he has for you.
Plans to give you peace and a future, to heal you and not to harm you.
Lovingly he calls to you, "Come, come, just as you are, for I love you."

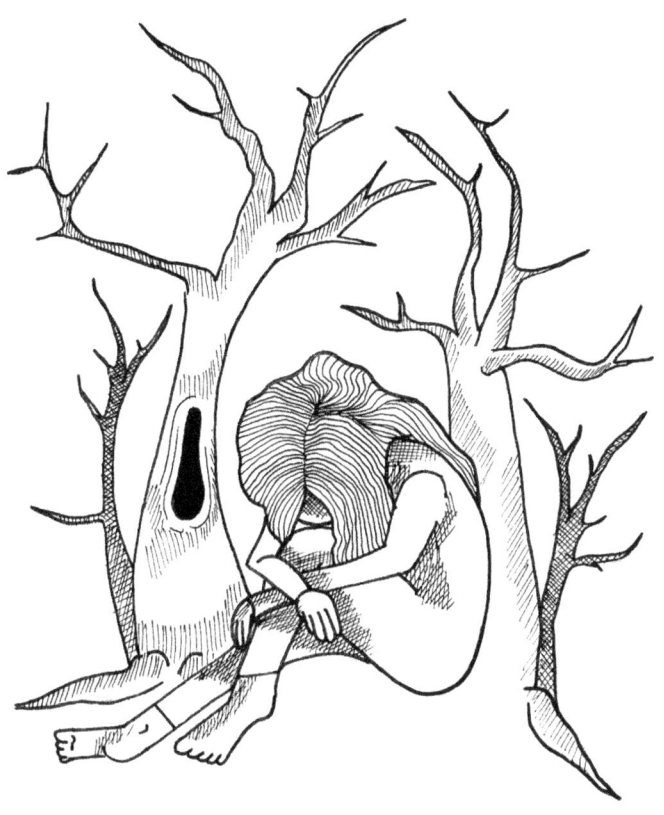

Thank You

Thank you for coming when I was feeling so sad.
Thank you for coming and making me feel glad.

Thank you for loving me, whether I'm fat or thin.
Thank you for loving me, whether I'm right or wrong.

Thank you for caring and loving each other.
Thank you for two sisters and a brother.

Thank you for helping me when I needed you so bad.
Thank you for being my Mum and Dad.

Toni xxx

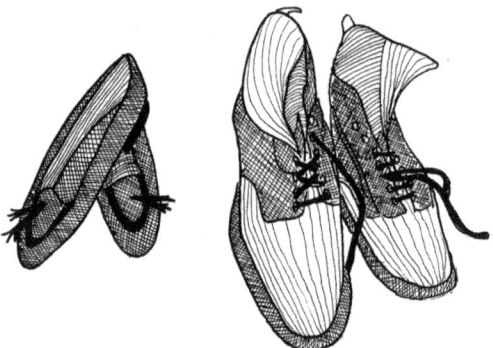

Smile

Where's the face that used to smile,
When I entered the room?
Now a scowl and gloomy look,
Because you do not feel loved.

Whose fault is that? Not mine, I know.
Tender loving kindness I long to give to you.
So stop being grumpy,
And see what a smile can do.

The Foolishness of Man – The Wisdom of God

How foolish of me to think that I can hide from you.
As in the garden of Eden, when you called, "Where are you?"
Giving me an opportunity to come to you and confess,
Confess and receive forgiveness,
Because of the blood of Jesus.

Only you, my loving Heavenly Father, could have in his heart,
A plan, a plan to restore mankind to himself.
From the moment of our first rebellion.
When the energy of our soul deceiving us, said,
That we can have our own wisdom.

Your word o God says, "If anyone lacks wisdom,
He should ask, and it will be given unto him."
He will incline his ear to hear the still, small voice of God.
Fear of the Lord is the beginning of knowledge.
But fools despise wisdom and discipline.
For Man's ways are in full view of the Lord.

See first the kingdom of God and his righteousness,
And all things will be added unto you.
"If you abide in me and my word abides in you.
You shall ask what you will, and it shall be done for you."

A Bruised Reed

From within a padded cell,
Christ is doing all things well.
Away from the madness round about,
My world is turning inside out.

"Be still", they say like they know best.
I only want a sodding rest.
Peace and rest, I scream within.
Dare I give it all to him.

This Christ, this Christ, the saviour king.

I let go, and I feel him close.
Holding me, holding me, I rest.
Although I do not understand,
I know that he has taken my hand.

Yes, I am surrendering my life to him.
His peace, his peace, I take my rest.

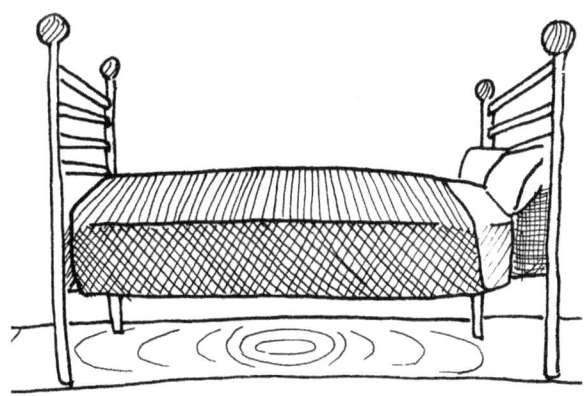

Blood

There is no forgiveness with the shedding of blood.
Life is in the blood.
Sin has to be paid for.
Death came by one man Adam and by the one man Jesus Christ.
Son of God, son of Man, Jesus Christ, comes salvation.

Give thanks to him, for he is worthy.
Worthy of all praise and glory, now and evermore.
Thank you, Father God, for our loving saviour.
With grateful hearts, we give you thanks.
Restore all things to yourself, for yours is the glory.
All heaven declares your glory.
Day after day for all to see.
How can anyone say there is no God,
When all nature shows your creation.
There is only one God, creator of Heaven and Earth.

Giver of all life.

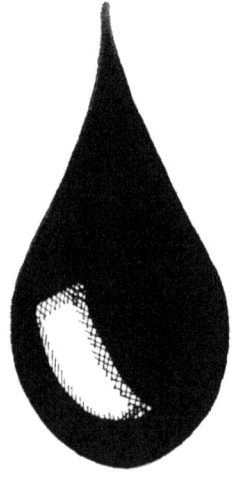

Paid For

Does it matter how it's said?
The world still wants my saviour dead.
Dead and gone and out of the way,
So the Devil doesn't have to pay.
When you're dead, you're dead! And that is that.
There ain't, there ain't no coming back.

Separated from the Father in his agony,
My loving Lord and saviour hanging on the tree.
Darkness covered him, our filth, sickness, shame.
Sin and death and every kind of pain.
Willingly he took upon himself,
For the victory, he'd gain.

Forgive then, forgive them, Father; they know not what they do.
May the glory, the glory, return, return to you.
"He's won, he's won", the angels shout.
Here comes the victory, the atonement paid for.
For you and for me. It is finished! It is finished!
Said he and committed up his spirit.

In the darkest moments, the Devil thought he'd won.
But oh no! Oh no!
His defeat had come.
Raised from the dead, how can it be?
We did nothing; he did it all.
The only acceptable sacrifice.

God's only begotten son.
So with humility and repentance.
Listen to him knock! Ask him into your heart.
His name is Jesus.
He is your Lord.

With You in Mind

What do you like in this world?
Do you like boxes? Do you like pearls?
Do you like the sun and rain?
Would you like to come back again?
Well, it is just a one-way trip.
No coming back; this is it.

The Earth is the Lord's and everything in it.
The world and all who live in it. That means you and me.
Because of him, we have our being.
He knitted you together in your mother's womb.
And he loves you, planned before the creation of the Earth,
Were you, in the mind of God.

Our all-knowing God knows the plans he has for you.
Something, something, only you can do.
Created for a purpose, part of his divine plan.
He sent his son Jesus, son of God, son of Man,
To save us from our sinfulness.
The helpless state we're in.

The answer's really simple: like a little child come,
Believe, receive the gift of love,
Through God's only begotten son.
Open up your heart and let the King of glory in.
Who is this King of glory?
The Lord Almighty, he is the King of glory.

Be Mine, I Know Your Name

How precious you are like a jewel,
When it reflects the light and shines.
Light is so much nicer than the darkness.
Let me hold you in the light of my love.
The moment I first saw you, my newborn child,
Behold, the Lord has blessed me.

How I praise his holy name, the giver of all life.
What are we, Lord, that you should care for us?
May praise and honour and glory be yours, now and evermore.
You make them male and female, and they became one,
Crowned with the gift of free will,
Your eternal love flows on and on.

Every knee will bow, and tongue confess,
That Jesus Christ is Lord, begotten, not created.
Through him, all things were made,
Without him, nothing was made that had not been made.
In him was life, and that life was the light of men.
That everyone who believes in him may have eternal life.

Perfectly Loved

Do you know you are perfectly loved?
Scum of the Earth brought forth in iniquity.
Do you not know you are perfectly loved?
God offers deliverance from the power of indwelling sin.
"Behold, you desire truth in the inward parts."
God will never compromise with sin.
Do you know you are perfectly loved?
Sent by the Father from Heaven above.

If I ascend into Heaven, you are there.
If I make my bed in Hell, behold, you are there.
If I take the wings of the morning,
And dwell in the uttermost parts of the sea,
Even there, your hand shall lead me.
If I say, "Surely the darkness shall fall on me",
Even the night shall be as light about me;
Indeed, the darkness shall not hide from you.

But the night shines as the day.
The darkness and light are both alike to you.
Help me to confess my sin, receive your forgiveness.
Be cleansed from within—the price paid in full.
By Jesus, my loving saviour. Raised from the dead.
His blood shed in crucifixion. Scoured, beaten,
Scorned, humiliated, spat on, cursed, mocked,
Laughed at, insulted, all this for me, a sinner.

Salvation is found in no one else.
For there is no other name under Heaven by which we must be saved.
Do you know you are perfectly loved?
Repent, ask for forgiveness; you were bought at a price by Jesus.

May your eyes be opened to see,
You are perfectly loved, eternally,
By the Father, the Son, and the Holy Spirit.
Receive and know that you are perfectly loved.

His Saving Grace

You are for us, Lord, and not against us.
It is not about us, but is for us,
That Jesus came to claim the victory.
Victory over the power of death.
For the wages of sin is death.
He who had no sin, the only begotten son of God.
Born to become our atonement and saviour.

Born of a virgin, conceived of the Holy Spirit,
Lived a sinless life, the light of the world.
No one comes to the Father except through him.
I am the resurrection and the life.
He who believes in me will live even though he dies.
Seek him with all your heart.
Repent, surrender; God wants that none should perish.

Lord Renew My Mind

Do you think you hear it?
The first time it is said.
Why this "A?", "What?", "Pardon?"
Are you walking with the dead?
Pay attention and gain understanding.
Listen, my son, to a father's instruction.
Receive Jesus and live.

Meditate on God's word day and night.
May his statutes be written on your heart.
Be still and know that he is God.
Spend time with your Heavenly Father.
He knows what is good for you.
With prayer, petition and thanksgiving,
Make your request known to the Lord.

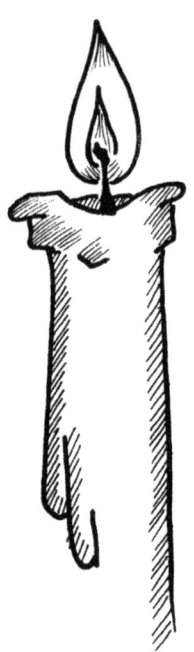

Hand in Hand

When I and me are on the throne of my heart,
I think I can go it on my own.
Then I discover weaknesses.
I have needs I cannot meet.
I humble myself. Why so hard?
Why so hard to humble myself?
Pride, a trap to ensnare us,
And who gets hurt? Ourselves.

How much is an opinion worth?
Enough to draw a sword.
Leaving someone wounded or dead.
With a hastily spoken word.
Hold still that lethal weapon.
Keep your mouth shut tight.
Let the heat of your opinion rest.
You are not always right.

Even a fool can look wise if he keeps quiet.
Let's reason together with kindness and understanding.
Encouraging each other in goodness.
Caring one for the other, then it will not be I and me.
Then it will be sharing, as it should be.
Peace and harmony are better than strife.
So with tender loving care, let's walk together,
Hand in hand.

Arise, Arise

All have fallen short of the glory of God.
So what do you do when you are guilty?
Look up at the cross; hang it there.
The price was paid in full.
So confess, cry out, the pain is real.
The pain of your forgiveness,
Carried by the son of God.

Open our eyes that we might see,
The wondrous thing, done by thee o Lord.
Really, really see, and be ever grateful.
Giving back the life we owe.
Serving and following you.
That we should love one another,
So the world will know that we are yours.

Nothing is hidden from you, my God.
I ask for your mercy; fill me with reverent fear.
For you are holy and worthy of praise.
May all honour and glory be yours.
Every knee will bow before you,
And confess Jesus Christ is Lord.
He will restore all things to the Father.

Think Not Higher Than You Ought

Help me not to be a pharisee,
And say thank God that was not me.
Making the mistake of thinking higher of myself
Than I ought; a pit we fall in.
Repent, knowing all sin is paid for by Jesus.

Thank you for your promise o, Lord.
The promise to finish what you have begun in me.
May I surrender my life to your rule o Lord.
Humble myself. I can do nothing of my own.
I cannot earn your love or a place in Heaven.
Thank you, Heavenly Father, for your son.

Jesus, Jesus, the only begotten son of God.
Died instead of me, nailed to the cross.
Crucified, buried, and risen from the dead.
The gift of salvation is available to men.
God wants that none should perish.
Accept it while you can.

Sisters

Sisters in Jesus,
Are Brenda and I.
When we're together,
The time really flies.

Sharing and caring,
Lifting our care to our Lord above.
Singing him praises,
Talking of his love.

Giving and sharing,
In things old and new.
Thanking our Jesus,
For each other too.

Sisters for eternity.

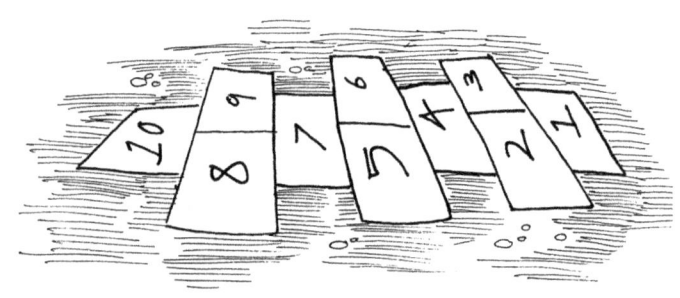

His Faithfulness

Did Jesus say, "I love you, But!"
The way I say to you?
Remember, he has not finished his work in me.
Faithfully every day, he leads me on and on.
Bids me to follow him, gives the Holy Spirit,
To comfort, guide, reveal his ways.

Forgiving is not easy; it cost Jesus his life.
Forgive them, forgive them; they know not what they do.
Have you ever thought of that?
When an action done against you was so deliberate.
They know not what they do; the pain is real.
As it was for him hanging on the tree.

Forgiveness is setting yourself free.
Free from the agony of the hurt you feel in remembering.
Remembering affliction in word or deed against you.
Forgive, lay it down; you can! The Lord will enable you,
And o the freedom in forgiveness from Jesus,
So you can forgive too.

Christ's prayer that we shall love one another,
So that the world will know that we are his.
Thank you, Father God,
For your only begotten son Jesus.
My precious Lord and saviour.
Amen.

Gems

There are gems in life, and you are one.
I've often seen you shine.

So many shades and colours,
Over space and time.

If I do not tell you, then how are you to know?
It's lovely to remember the joy, the tears, the fun.

The excitement of a race when it's first begun.
For gems do not just happen; they are created, as you know.

I'm proud I had a part in it; I just thought I'd tell you so.

Forgetting what lies behind, running the race to win.
Nothing is impossible with God.

www.ingramcontent.com/pod-product-compliance
Lightning Source LLC
Chambersburg PA
CBHW061301040426
42444CB00010B/2453

Found is a heartfelt collection of poems written by a survivor of long-term domestic abuse when she became fortified by faith and eventually found the power to flee. The poems are reflections of the sadness of enduring pain combined with the joy of finding peace, love, and belonging in the arms of God.

T. M. Mackie is a mother, daughter, and sister. She is eighty-one years old and a survivor of long-term interpersonal abuse. She currently resides in East Lothian, Scotland, UK.

COVER DESIGN: JONATHAN HILL
www.wipfandstock.com

Resource Publications
An imprint of *Wipf and Stock Publishers*

ISBN 978-1-6667-4219-0

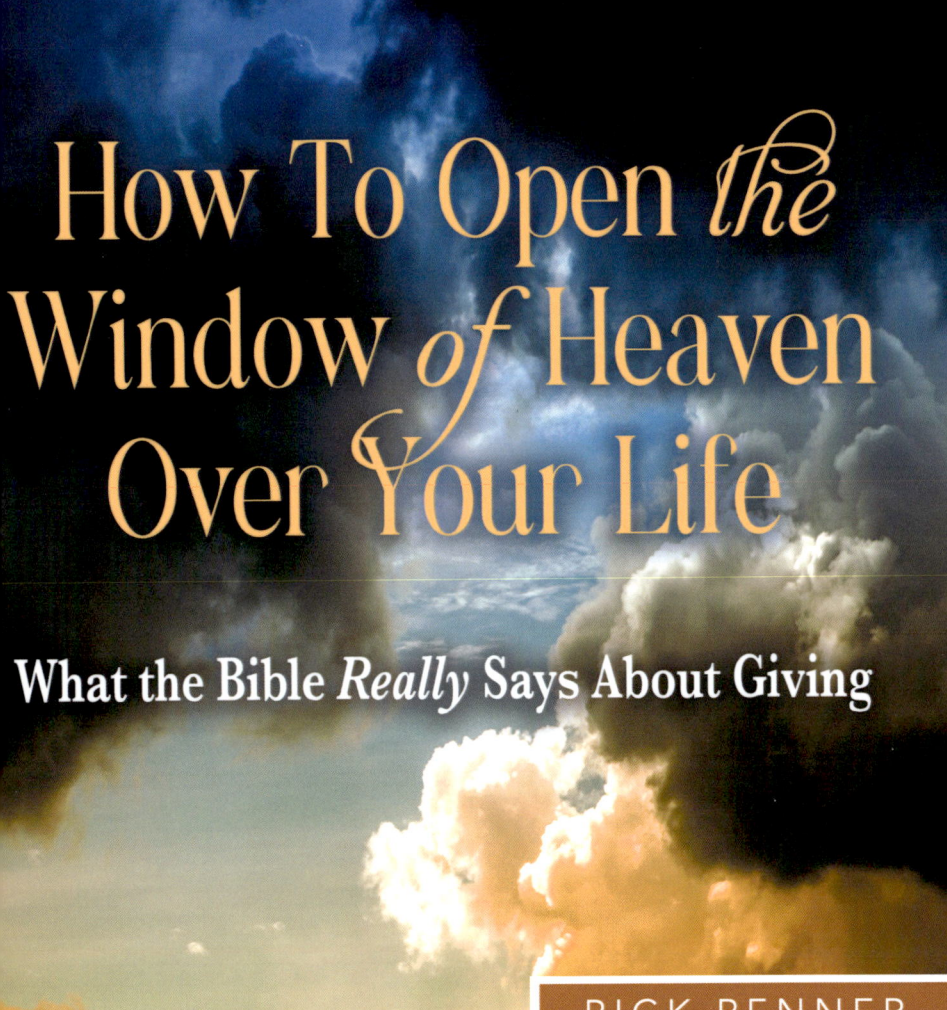

What does the Bible say about giving? Is it really necessary for us to give, and does it truly have the power to transform our lives? In this five-part series, Rick Renner will show you how to open the window of Heaven over your life through generosity and sacrificial giving. Listing examples from the Old and New Testaments as well as from his personal life, Rick plainly reveals how the principles of giving outlined in Scripture still apply to our lives today. Discover with this foundational series how abundantly God wants to move in your life and meet your needs.

A Note From Rick Renner

I am on a personal quest to see a "revival of the Bible" so people can establish their lives on a firm foundation that will stand strong and endure the test as end-time storm winds begin to intensify.

In order to experience a revival of the Bible in your personal life, it is important to take time each day to read, receive, and apply its truths to your life. James tells us that if we will continue in the perfect law of liberty — refusing to be forgetful hearers, but determined to be doers — we will be blessed in our ways. As you watch or listen to the programs in this series and work through this corresponding study guide, I trust you will search the Scriptures and allow the Holy Spirit to help you hear something new from God's Word that applies specifically to your life. I encourage you to be a doer of the Word He reveals to you. Whatever the cost, I assure you — it will be worth it.

> Thy words were found, and I did eat them;
> and thy word was unto me the joy and rejoicing of mine heart:
> for I am called by thy name, O Lord God of hosts.
> — Jeremiah 15:16

Your brother and friend in Jesus Christ,

Rick Renner

Rick Renner

Unless otherwise indicated, all scripture quotations are taken from the *King James Version* of the Bible.

Scripture quotations marked (*ESV*) are from *The Holy Bible, English Standard Version*. ESV® Text Edition: 2016. Copyright © 2001 by Crossway Bibles, a publishing ministry of Good News Publishers.

Scripture quotations marked (*NIV*) are taken from the *Holy Bible, New International Version*®, *NIV*® Copyright ©1973, 1978, 1984, 2011 by Biblica, Inc.® Used by permission. All rights reserved worldwide.

Scripture quotations marked (*NLT*) are taken from the Holy Bible, *New Living Translation*, copyright © 1996, 2004, 2015 by Tyndale House Foundation. Used by permission of Tyndale House Publishers, Inc., Carol Stream, Illinois 60188. All rights reserved.

How To Open the Window of Heaven Over Your Life
What the Bible Really Says About Giving

Copyright © 2022 by Rick Renner
P.O. Box 702040
Tulsa, OK 74170

Published by Rick Renner Ministries
www.renner.org

ISBN 13: 978-1-6675-0023-2

eBook ISBN 13: 978-1-6675-0024-9

All rights reserved. No portion of this book may be reproduced or transmitted in any form or by any means — electronic, mechanical, photocopy, recording, scanning, or other — except for brief quotations in critical reviews or articles, without the prior written permission of the Publisher.